**Published By Adam Gilbin**

@ Leroy Artis

Carnivore Diet: No Sugar and Fruit, Just Meat

From Pure Carnivorous Cuisine

**All Right RESERVED**

ISBN 978-87-94477-70-3

# TABLE OF CONTENTS

Turkey Chili With Avocado ................................................. 1

Salmon Fillet With Roasted Asparagus ........................... 4

Grilled Steak With Roasted Vegetables........................... 6

Hamwrapped Asparagus ................................................. 8

Salmon Carpaccio With Horseradish Cream ................ 10

Baconwrapped Shrimp Skewers.................................... 12

Grilled Rib Eye Steak...................................................... 14

Buttergarlic Shrimp Skewers......................................... 16

Lamb Chops With Rosemary ......................................... 18

Pork Ribs With Dry Rub ................................................. 20

Chicken Thighs With Herbs ........................................... 21

Scrambled Eggs With Bacon And Sausage .................... 24

Steak And Eggs With A Side Of Mushrooms ................. 26

Ground Beef And Spinach Omelet ................................ 28

Bacon Wrapped Asparagus With A Side Of Boiled Eggs. 30

Sausage And Cheese Omelet......................................... 32

Chicken And Vegetable Skillet....................................... 34

Ground Beef Breakfast Skillet ........................................ 36

Egg And Bacon Breakfast Muffins ................................. 38

Egg And Cheese Sandwich.............................................. 40

Bacon, Egg, And Cheese Biscuit...................................... 42

Sausage And Egg Breakfast Burrito ............................... 43

Classic Bacon Wrapped Asparagus Spears..................... 45

Garlic Parmesan Bacon Wrapped Asparagus Spears ..... 47

Balsamic Glazed Bacon Wrapped Asparagus Spears...... 49

Grilled Salmon With Asparagus...................................... 51

Egg And Bacon Salad ...................................................... 53

Grilled Steak And Vegetables ........................................ 55

Turkey Burger With Avocado ......................................... 57

Turkey Meatballs In Tomato Sauce ............................... 59

Pan Fried Pork Chops With Mustard Cream Sauce ........ 62

Grilled Chicken Caesar Salad ......................................... 64

Tuna Avocado Lettuce Wraps: ....................................... 66

Ground Beef Lettuce Wraps........................................... 67

Chicken Bacon Ranch Salad............................................ 69

Beef Patties ..................................................... 70

Simple Beef Roast............................................ 72

Roasted Sirloin Steak....................................... 73

Beef Tacos ....................................................... 75

Bacon Mayonnaise ........................................... 76

Duck Fat Mayonnaise ....................................... 78

Easy Hollandaise Sauce ................................... 80

Ovenboiled Eggs .............................................. 82

Perfect Bacon .................................................. 83

Crispy Baked Chicken Wings With Red Cabbage Slaw ... 84

Baked Salmon With Avocado Salsa ................. 86

Pan Seared Pork Chops With Garlic And Herbs.............. 88

Zucchini Rolls With Ham And Cheese.............. 90

Cooked Ham With Fresh Figs .......................... 92

Grilled Sausages With Mustard ....................... 93

Bacon And Cheese Omelet............................... 95

Cauliflower Rice............................................... 96

Baconwrapped Asparagus................................ 98

| | |
|---|---|
| Creamed Spinach | 100 |
| Bacon Wrapped Pork Chops | 102 |
| Slow Cooked Beef Brisket | 104 |
| Herb Crusted Lamb Chops | 107 |
| Steak And Egg Breakfast Salad | 109 |
| Bun Less Bacon Cheeseburger | 111 |
| Salmon And Cream Cheese Breakfast Wrap | 113 |
| Grilled Steak With Roasted Vegetables | 115 |
| Baked Lemon Herb Chicken | 117 |
| Salmon With Lemon Dill Sauce | 119 |
| Beef Stir Fry With Vegetables | 121 |
| Crispy Baked Chicken Wings | 124 |
| Bbq Ribs | 126 |
| Grilled Sausages | 128 |
| Classic Rib Eye Lettuce Wraps | 130 |
| Garlic Butter Rib Eye Lettuce Wraps | 132 |
| Asian Inspired Rib Eye Lettuce Wraps | 135 |
| Bacon Wrapped Dates | 138 |

Deviled Eggs With Bacon ............................................... 139

Garlic Butter Shrimp ..................................................... 141

Grilled Chicken Caesar Salad With Bacon .................... 142

## Turkey Chili With Avocado

**Ingredients:**

- 1 pound ground turkey
- 1 tablespoon chili powder
- 2 teaspoons ground cumin
- 1 teaspoon smoked paprika
- 1/2 teaspoon dried oregano
- 1 teaspoon sea salt
- 1/2 teaspoon freshly ground black pepper
- 1 (15 ounce) can black beans, drained and rinsed
- 1 tablespoon olive oil

- 1 onion, diced

- 1 red bell pepper, diced

- 2 cloves garlic, minced

- 1 (14.5 ounce) can diced tomatoes

- 2 cups chicken broth

- 1 avocado, diced

- Optional toppings: fresh cilantro, diced jalapeno, sour cream, grated cheese

**Directions:**

1. Heat the olive oil in a large pot over medium heat. Add the onion and bell pepper and cook until softened, about 5 minutes.
2. Add the garlic, ground turkey, chili powder, cumin, paprika, oregano, salt, and pepper. Cook, stirring frequently, until the turkey is cooked through, about 8 minutes.

3. Add the beans, tomatoes, and chicken broth. Bring

## Salmon Fillet With Roasted Asparagus

**Ingredients:**

- 2 tablespoons olive oil
- Salt and pepper to taste
- 1 bunch asparagus
- 4 salmon fillets
- 2 tablespoons lemon juice

**Directions:**

1. Preheat oven to 400 degrees F.
2. Place the salmon fillets on a baking sheet lined with parchment paper.
3. Drizzle the salmon fillets with olive oil and season with salt and pepper.
4. Roast the salmon in the preheated oven for 15 minutes.

5. Meanwhile, prepare the asparagus by removing the woody ends and tossing with lemon juice, salt, and pepper.
6. Place the asparagus on the same baking sheet with the salmon, making sure the asparagus is not overlapping with the salmon.
7. Roast the asparagus for an additional 10 minutes.
8. Remove from the oven and serve the salmon and asparagus together.

# Grilled Steak With Roasted Vegetables

**Ingredients:**

- Steak (12 lbs)

- Olive oil

- Salt and pepper

- Assorted vegetables (e.g. bell peppers, onions, mushrooms, zucchini, eggplant)

**Directions:**
1. Preheat the grill to mediumhigh heat.
2. Rub the steak with olive oil and season with salt and pepper.
3. Place the steak on the hot grill and cook for 45 minutes per side, or until it reaches your desired doneness.

4. Meanwhile, prepare the vegetables. Slice them into equal sizes and toss with olive oil, salt, and pepper.
5. Once the steak is done, remove it from the grill and let it rest.
6. Place the vegetables on the grill and cook until tender, about 35 minutes per side.
7. Slice the steak and serve with the roasted vegetables. Enjoy!

# Hamwrapped Asparagus

**Ingredients:**

- 16 fresh asparagus
- 8 slices of prosciutto
- Olive oil
- Salt and pepper to taste.

**Directions:**

1. Preheat the oven to 200°C. Take a bunch of asparagus and cut away the woody parts at the base of the stems.
2. Wrap each asparagus with half a slice of prosciutto, starting from the base to the tip.
3. Arrange the prosciutto wrapped asparagus on a baking sheet and season with a drizzle of olive oil, salt, and pepper. Bake the baking sheet in the preheated oven and cook the

asparagus for about 10 to 12 minutes, until the ham becomes crispy and the asparagus is tender.
4. Once cooked, transfer the ham wrapped asparagus to a serving platter and serve hot. Prosciutto wrapped asparagus is delicious as an appetizer or side dish.
5. You can accompany this preparation with a sauce made with mayonnaise, mustard, or melted butter if you wish to further enrich the flavor.

# Salmon Carpaccio With Horseradish Cream

**Ingredients:**

- Olive oil

- Salt and pepper to taste

- 2 tablespoons horseradish cream

- 200 g thinly sliced smoked salmon

- Lemon juice

- Chopped fresh parsley (for garnish)

**Directions:**

1. Arrange the slices of smoked salmon on a serving platter. Squeeze lemon juice over the salmon and season with a drizzle of olive oil, salt, and pepper.
2. In a small bowl, mix the horseradish cream with a teaspoon of lemon juice. Pour the

horseradish cream over the salmon Carpaccio, spreading it evenly.
3. Garnish the dish with fresh chopped parsley. Serve salmon Carpaccio with horseradish cream as an appetizer or light main course.

# Baconwrapped Shrimp Skewers

**Ingredients:**

- Olive oil
- Salt and pepper to taste
- Skewers or toothpicks
- 16 fresh shrimp, shelled and gutted
- 8 slices of bacon
- Lemon juice

**Directions:**

1. Preheat the oven grill or barbecue. Wrap each shrimp with half a slice of bacon.
2. Thread the bacon wrapped shrimp into skewers or toothpicks. Season the skewers with lemon juice, olive oil, salt, and pepper.

3. Cook the bacon wrapped shrimp skewers under the oven grill or on the barbecue grill for about 8 to 10 minutes, turning them occasionally, until the bacon is crispy and the shrimp are cooked through.
4. Once cooked, transfer the bacon wrapped shrimp skewers to a serving platter and serve hot.

## Grilled Rib Eye Steak

**Ingredients:**

- 2 teaspoons garlic powder
- 2 teaspoons onion powder
- 2 Rib eye steaks (about 8 oz each)
- 2 tablespoons olive oil
- Salt and pepper to taste

**Directions:**

1. Preheat your grill to high heat.
2. Brush both sides of the rib eye steaks with olive oil.
3. Season the steaks with garlic powder, onion powder, salt, and pepper.

4. Place the steaks on the hot grill and cook to your desired level of doneness, typically 46 minutes per side for medium rare.
5. Remove the Grilled Rib eye Steaks from the grill and let them rest for a few minutes before slicing. Enjoy these juicy and flavorful steaks!

## Buttergarlic Shrimp Skewers

**Ingredients:**

- 2 garlic cloves, minced

- 2 tablespoons chopped fresh parsley

- Salt and pepper to taste

- Metal or wooden skewers (if using wooden skewers, soak them in water for 30 minutes before using)

- 1 lb large shrimp, peeled and deveined

- 4 tablespoons butter, melted

**Directions:**
1. Preheat your grill to medium high heat.
2. In a bowl, mix the melted butter, minced garlic, chopped parsley, salt, and pepper to create the marinade.

3. Thread the peeled and deveined shrimp onto the metal or soaked wooden skewers.
4. Brush the shrimp skewers with the buttergarlic marinade, coating them evenly.
5. Grill the shrimp skewers on the preheated grill for 23 minutes per side or until they are pink and opaque.
6. Remove the Butter Garlic Shrimp Skewers from the grill and serve immediately. Enjoy these succulent and garlicky delights!

## Lamb Chops With Rosemary

**Ingredients:**

- 2 tablespoons olive oil
- 2 tablespoons fresh rosemary leaves, chopped
- 4 lamb chops
- Salt and pepper to taste

**Directions:**
1. Preheat your grill or a grill pan to mediumhigh heat.
2. Brush both sides of the lamb chops with olive oil.
3. Season the lamb chops with chopped fresh rosemary, salt, and pepper, pressing the herbs gently onto the meat.
4. Place the seasoned lamb chops on the hot grill and cook them to your preferred level of

doneness, about 34 minutes per side for mediumrare.

5. Remove the Lamb Chops with Rosemary from the grill and let them rest for a few minutes before serving. Enjoy these tender and aromatic lamb chops!

## Pork Ribs With Dry Rub

**Ingredients:**

- 2 tablespoons onion powder

- 2 tablespoons ground black pepper

- 1 tablespoon salt

- 1 tablespoon ground cumin

- 2 lbs pork spare ribs

- 2 tablespoons paprika

- 2 tablespoons garlic powder

- 1 tablespoon chili powder

**Directions:**

1. Preheat your oven to 300°F (150°C).

2. In a small bowl, mix the paprika, garlic powder, onion powder, black pepper, salt, cumin, and chili powder to create the dry rub.
3. Rub the dry spice mixture evenly over the pork ribs, covering all sides.
4. Place the seasoned pork ribs on a baking sheet lined with aluminum foil.
5. Cover the ribs with another layer of foil, sealing the edges to create a packet.
6. Bake the Pork Ribs with Dry Rub in the preheated oven for 2.53 hours or until the meat is tender and pulls away from the bones easily.
7. Remove the foil and place the ribs back in the oven for an additional 1015 minutes to crisp up the surface.
8. Serve the flavorful and tender Pork Ribs with Dry Rub, and enjoy the fingerlicking goodness!

**Chicken Thighs With Herbs**

**Ingredients:**

- 1 tablespoon chopped fresh thyme
- 1 tablespoon chopped fresh rosemary
- 1 tablespoon chopped fresh sage
- 4 bonein, skinon chicken thighs
- 2 tablespoons olive oil
- Salt and pepper to taste

**Directions:**

1. Preheat your oven to 400°F (200°C).
2. In a bowl, mix the olive oil, chopped thyme, rosemary, and sage to create the herb marinade.
3. Rub the herb marinade evenly over the chicken thighs, including under the skin.
4. Season the chicken thighs with salt and pepper.

5. Place the seasoned chicken thighs on a baking sheet lined with parchment paper, skin side up.
6. Bake the Chicken Thighs with Herbs in the preheated oven for 3035 minutes or until the chicken is cooked through and the skin is crispy.
7. Remove the chicken thighs from the oven and let them rest for a few minutes before serving. Enjoy the fragrant and flavorful chicken thighs!

## Scrambled Eggs With Bacon And Sausage

**INGREDIENTS:**

- 2 sausages, chopped
- Salt and pepper, to taste
- 2 tablespoons of butter
- 4 eggs
- 2 strips of bacon, chopped

**DIRECTIONS:**

1. In a skillet over medium heat, cook the chopped bacon and sausages until browned and crisp. Remove from the pan and set aside.
2. In a bowl, whisk the eggs until well beaten. Season with salt and pepper.
3. In the same skillet over low heat, melt the butter. Add the beaten eggs and stir

constantly with a spatula until the eggs start to set.
4. Add the cooked bacon and sausage back into the skillet with the eggs and continue to stir until the eggs are cooked to your desired consistency.
5. Serve hot with additional salt and pepper to taste.
6. Note: If you're following a strict carnivore diet, make sure to use highquality, grassfed bacon and sausage without any fillers or additives. You can also add other meats such as ham or steak to this dish for variety.

## Steak And Eggs With A Side Of Mushrooms

**INGREDIENTS:**

- 1 pound mushrooms, sliced
- 2 garlic cloves, minced
- 2 tablespoons butter
- 2 steaks (Rib eye , sirloin, or your preferred cut)
- 4 eggs
- Salt and pepper, to taste

**Directions:**
1. Preheat a large skillet over mediumhigh heat.
2. Season the steaks with salt and pepper on both sides.
3. Add the steaks to the skillet and cook for 45 minutes on each side or until desired

doneness is achieved. Remove from the skillet and set aside.
4. In the same skillet, add the sliced mushrooms and minced garlic. Cook until the mushrooms are tender and golden brown, about 57 minutes. Season with salt and pepper.
5. In another skillet, melt 1 tablespoon of butter over mediumhigh heat.
6. Crack the eggs into the skillet and cook until the whites are set and the yolks are still runny, about 23 minutes.
7. Divide the steaks and mushrooms between two plates.
8. Place two eggs on top of each plate.
9. Garnish with chopped parsley or chives if desired.
10. Serve immediately and enjoy your delicious steak and eggs with a side of mushrooms!

## Ground Beef And Spinach Omelet

**INGREDIENTS:**

- 2 cups fresh spinach, chopped
- 1/4 cup shredded cheddar cheese
- Salt and pepper to taste
- 4 eggs
- 1/4 cup milk
- 1/2 pound ground beef
- 2 tablespoons butter or oil

**DIRECTIONS:**

1. In a large mixing bowl, whisk together the eggs and milk until well combined. Set aside.

2. In a large skillet over mediumhigh heat, brown the ground beef until fully cooked. Drain any excess fat.
3. Add the chopped spinach to the skillet and cook until wilted, stirring occasionally.
4. Pour the egg mixture into the skillet, tilting the skillet to distribute the eggs evenly. Cook until the edges start to set, then use a spatula to gently lift the edges and allow the uncooked eggs to flow underneath.
5. When the eggs are almost set, sprinkle the shredded cheese over one half of the omelet.
6. Use a spatula to fold the other half of the omelet over the cheese and cook for another minute or two, until the cheese is melted and the eggs are fully cooked.
7. Season with salt and pepper to taste, and serve hot.
8. Enjoy your delicious ground beef and spinach omelet, perfect for a carnivorous diet!

## Bacon Wrapped Asparagus With A Side Of Boiled Eggs

**INGREDIENTS:**

- 8 slices of bacon

- 4 eggs

- 1 lb asparagus spears, trimmed

- Salt and pepper to taste

**DIRECTIONS:**

1. Preheat the oven to 400°F (200°C).
2. Wash and trim the asparagus spears, then pat them dry.
3. Divide the asparagus into 8 even bundles.
4. Wrap each bundle of asparagus with a slice of bacon, starting at the bottom and spiraling up to the top.

5. Place the bacon wrapped asparagus bundles on a baking sheet lined with parchment paper.
6. Bake for 2025 minutes or until the bacon is crispy and the asparagus is tender.
7. While the asparagus is baking, boil the eggs. Place the eggs in a saucepan and cover them with cold water. Bring the water to a boil over high heat, then reduce the heat to low and let the eggs simmer for 10 minutes.
8. Once the eggs are done, remove them from the saucepan and let them cool before peeling.
9. Season the eggs with salt and pepper to taste.
10. Serve the bacon wrapped asparagus alongside the boiled eggs.
11. Enjoy your delicious and satisfying carnivore friendly meal!

# Sausage And Cheese Omelet

**Ingredients:**

- 23 sausages, sliced
- 2 large eggs
- Salt and pepper
- 1/4 cup shredded cheese
- Butter

**Directions:**

1. Preheat a skillet over low heat.
2. Put the sliced sausages to the skillet and cook for about 23 minutes on each side, or until tender.
3. Remove the sausages from the skillet and set aside.
4. In a bowl, beat two eggs with salt and pepper.

5. Melt a tablespoon of butter in the same skillet over medium heat.
6. Pour the beaten eggs into the skillet and let them cook for 12 minutes.
7. Add the cooked sausages and shredded cheese to one half of the omelet.
8. Use a spatula to fold the other half of the omelet over the sausages and cheese.
9. Cook for another minute, or until the cheese is melted.
10. Serve the omelet hot.

# Chicken And Vegetable Skillet

**Ingredients:**

- 1/4 onion, diced
- 2 cloves garlic, minced
- Salt and pepper
- 4 oz. cooked chicken breast, diced
- 1/2 bell pepper, diced
- Butter

**Directions:**
1. Preheat a skillet over low heat.
2. Melt a tablespoon of butter in the skillet.
3. Add the diced bell pepper, onion, and garlic to the skillet and cook for 23 minutes, or until softened.

4. Add the diced chicken breast to the skillet and season with salt and pepper.
5. Cook for another 23 minutes, or until the chicken is heated through.
6. Serve hot.

## Ground Beef Breakfast Skillet

**Ingredients:**

- 1/4 onion, diced

- 1/2 bell pepper, diced

- 8 oz. ground beef

- Salt and pepper

- Butter

**Directions:**
1. Preheat a skillet over low heat.
2. Melt one tablespoon of butter in the skillet.
3. Add the diced onion and bell pepper to the skillet and cook for 23 minutes, or until softened.
4. Put the ground beef to the skillet and season with salt and pepper.

5. Cook the ground beef, breaking it up with a spatula, until browned and cooked through, about 810 minutes.
6. Serve hot.

# Egg And Bacon Breakfast Muffins

**Ingredients:**

- 6 eggs

- Salt and pepper

- 12 slices of bacon

- Butter or oil for greasing muffin tin

**Directions:**

1. Preheat the oven to 375°F (190°C).
2. Grease a 6cup muffin tin with butter or oil.
3. Cut the bacon slices in half and line the muffin cups with the bacon, making sure to cover the bottom and sides of each cup.
4. Crack an egg into each baconlined cup.
5. Season each egg with salt and pepper.
6. Bake the muffins for 2025 minutes, or until the bacon is crispy and the egg whites are set.

7. Remove the muffins from the oven and let cool for a few minutes before using a knife to loosen the edges and removing them from the muffin tin.
8. Serve hot.

# Egg And Cheese Sandwich

**Ingredients:**

- 2 slices of cheese
- 2 slices of bread
- 2 eggs, scrambled
- Butter, for spreading

**Directions:**
1. Heat a skillet on medium heat.
2. Crack the eggs in a bowl and whisk until scrambled.
3. Pour eggs into the skillet and cook until done.
4. Spread butter on one side of each slice of bread.
5. Place the cheese slices on one slice of bread.
6. Add the scrambled eggs on top of the cheese.
7. Place the other slice of bread on top.

8. Grill the sandwich in the skillet for about 2 minutes per side or until the bread is golden and the cheese is melted.

# Bacon, Egg, And Cheese Biscuit

**Ingredients:**

- 4 slices of bacon, cooked
- 1 biscuit
- 2 eggs, scrambled
- 1 slice of cheese

**Directions:**
1. Preheat the oven to 350°F.
2. Line a baking sheet with parchment paper.
3. Place the biscuit on the baking sheet.
4. Spread the scrambled eggs over the biscuit.
5. Place the bacon slices on top of the eggs.
6. Top with the cheese slice.
7. Bake for 1015 minutes or until the cheese is melted and the biscuit is golden.

## Sausage And Egg Breakfast Burrito

**Ingredients:**

- 2 sausage patties, cooked
- 1 burrito sized tortilla
- 1/4 cup shredded cheese
- 2 eggs, scrambled
- Salsa, for topping (optional)

**Directions:**
1. Heat a skillet over medium heat.
2. Add the eggs to the skillet and scramble until done.
3. Place the burrito sized tortilla on a plate.
4. Layer the scrambled eggs, sausage patties, and cheese in the middle.

5. Fold the sides of the tortilla over the filling and roll it up.
6. Heat the burrito in the skillet for 2 minutes per side or until the tortilla is lightly browned.
7. Serve with your favorite salsa, if desired.

## Classic Bacon Wrapped Asparagus Spears

**Ingredients:**

- Olive oil or melted animal fat (for brushing)
- Salt and pepper to taste
- Fresh asparagus spears (thicker spears work best)
- Thinly sliced bacon strips

**Directions:**
1. Preheat your oven to 425°F (220°C).
2. Trim the tough ends of the asparagus spears, leaving the tender parts intact.
3. Divide the asparagus into bundles, consisting of 34 spears each, and wrap a bacon strip around each bundle, securing the bacon with the asparagus spears.

4. Place the bacon wrapped asparagus bundles on a baking sheet lined with parchment paper.
5. Brush the bacon wrapped asparagus spears with olive oil or melted animal fat for added flavor and to prevent them from sticking to the baking sheet.
6. Season the bundles with salt and pepper to taste.
7. Roast the bacon wrapped asparagus spears in the preheated oven for approximately 1520 minutes or until the bacon becomes crispy and the asparagus is tender.
8. Remove the bundles from the oven and let them cool slightly before serving.
9. Enjoy the classic bacon wrapped asparagus spears as an appetizing and nutrient packed snack or side dish.

## Garlic Parmesan Bacon Wrapped Asparagus Spears

**Ingredients:**

- Olive oil or melted animal fat (for brushing)
- Garlic powder
- Grated Parmesan cheese
- Fresh asparagus spears (thicker spears work best)
- Thinly sliced bacon strips
- Salt and pepper to taste

**Directions:**
1. Preheat your oven to 425°F (220°C).
2. Trim the tough ends of the asparagus spears, leaving the tender parts intact.

3. Divide the asparagus into bundles, consisting of 34 spears each, and wrap a bacon strip around each bundle, securing the bacon with the asparagus spears.
4. Place the bacon wrapped asparagus bundles on a baking sheet lined with parchment paper.
5. Brush the bacon wrapped asparagus spears with olive oil or melted animal fat, infusing them with extra flavor.
6. Sprinkle garlic powder, grated Parmesan cheese, salt, and pepper over the bundles, ensuring even distribution.
7. Roast the bacon wrapped asparagus spears in the preheated oven for approximately 1520 minutes or until the bacon becomes crispy and the asparagus is tender.
8. Remove the bundles from the oven and let them cool slightly before serving.

9. Relish the garlic parmesan bacon wrapped asparagus spears as an exquisite and flavorful appetizer or side dish.

## Balsamic Glazed Bacon Wrapped Asparagus Spears

**Ingredients:**

- Olive oil or melted animal fat (for brushing)

- Balsamic vinegar

- Fresh asparagus spears (thicker spears work best)

- Thinly sliced bacon strips

- Sea salt and freshly ground black pepper to taste

**Directions:**

1. Preheat your oven to 425°F (220°C).

2. Trim the tough ends of the asparagus spears, leaving the tender parts intact.
3. Divide the asparagus into bundles, consisting of 34 spears each, and wrap a bacon strip around each bundle, securing the bacon with the asparagus spears.
4. Place the bacon wrapped asparagus bundles on a baking sheet lined with parchment paper.
5. Brush the bacon wrapped asparagus spears with olive oil or melted animal fat, adding a hint of richness.
6. Drizzle balsamic vinegar over the bundles, creating a luscious glaze that complements the flavors of the bacon and asparagus.
7. Season the bundles with sea salt and freshly ground black pepper to enhance their taste.
8. Roast the bacon wrapped asparagus spears in the preheated oven for approximately 1520

minutes or until the bacon becomes crispy and the asparagus is tender.
9. Remove the bundles from the oven and let them cool slightly before serving.
10. Savor the balsamic glazed bacon wrapped asparagus spears as a delectable and sophisticated appetizer or side dish.

## Grilled Salmon With Asparagus

**Ingredients:**

- 2 tablespoons olive oil

- Salt and pepper, to taste

- 1 bunch asparagus

- 2 salmon fillets

- 1 lemon, cut into wedges

**Directions:**

1. Preheat the grill to mediumhigh heat.
2. Rub the salmon fillets with the olive oil, and season with salt and pepper.
3. Grill the salmon for 5 minutes per side, or until cooked through.
4. In the meanwhile, season the asparagus with salt & chilli after gently oiling it.
5. Grill the asparagus for 45 minutes, or until tender.
6. Remove from the heat and serve the salmon and asparagus with the lemon wedges.

## Egg And Bacon Salad

**Ingredients:**

- 1/2 cup mayonnaise
- 2 tablespoons chopped chives
- 1 tablespoon Dijon mustard
- Salt and pepper, to taste
- 6 slices bacon, cooked and crumbled
- 6 hard boiled eggs, chopped
- 4 cups baby spinach

**Directions:**
1. In a large bowl, combine the bacon, eggs, mayonnaise, chives, and mustard.
2. Season with salt and pepper, and mix until combined.

3. Add the baby spinach to the bowl and toss to combine.
4. Serve the salad immediately.

## Grilled Steak And Vegetables

**Ingredients:**

- Salt and pepper, to taste

- 1 bell pepper, sliced

- 1 red onion, sliced

- 2 steaks (any cut)

- 2 tablespoons olive oil

- 1 zucchini, sliced

**Directions:**
1. Preheat the grill to mediumhigh heat.
2. Sprinkle salt & chilli over the steaks after rubbing them with olive oil.
3. Grill the steaks for 46 minutes per side, or until cooked to desired doneness.

4. Meanwhile, lightly oil the vegetables and season with salt and pepper.
5. Grill the vegetables for 34 minutes, or until tender.
6. Remove from the heat and serve the steaks and vegetables.

## Turkey Burger With Avocado

**Ingredients:**

- 1 teaspoon dried oregano

- Salt and pepper, to taste

- 1 ripe avocado, sliced

- 4 hamburger buns

- 2 pounds ground turkey

- 2 tablespoons olive oil

- 2 cloves garlic, minced

**Directions:**

1. Preheat the grill to medium high heat.
2. In a large bowl, combine the ground turkey, olive oil, garlic, oregano, and salt and pepper.
3. Form the mixture into 4 patties.

4. Grill the burgers for 45 minutes per side, or until cooked through.
5. Serve the burgers on the hamburger buns with the sliced avocado.

## Turkey Meatballs In Tomato Sauce

**Ingredients:**

- 2 cloves garlic, minced

- 1 large egg

- 1 teaspoon dried oregano

- 1 teaspoon dried basil

- 1/2 teaspoon salt

- 1/4 teaspoon black pepper

- 1 tablespoon olive oil

- 1 can (14 oz) crushed tomatoes

- 1/2 teaspoon dried thyme

- 1 lb ground turkey

- 1/4 cup almond flour

- 1/4 cup grated Parmesan cheese

- 1/4 cup chopped fresh parsley

- 1/4 cup chopped onion

- 1/2 teaspoon dried rosemary

- Fresh basil leaves, chopped (for garnish)

**Directions:**

1. In a large bowl, combine ground turkey, almond flour, grated Parmesan cheese, chopped parsley, chopped onion, minced garlic, egg, dried oregano, dried basil, salt, and black pepper. Mix until well combined.
2. Shape the mixture into meatballs, approximately 11.5 inches in diameter.
3. The olive oil should be heated In a skillet set over medium heat.

4. Add the meatballs to the skillet and cook for about 45 minutes, turning occasionally, until browned on all sides.
5. In a separate saucepan, combine crushed tomatoes, dried thyme, and dried rosemary. The sauce should then be simmered for about 10 minutes over low heat.
6. Transfer the meatballs to the saucepan with the tomato sauce, ensuring they are submerged. Cover and simmer for an additional 1015 minutes until the meatballs are cooked through.
7. Garnish with fresh chopped basil before serving.

## Pan Fried Pork Chops With Mustard Cream Sauce

**Ingredients:**

- 2 tablespoons olive oil
- 1/2 cup heavy cream
- 2 tablespoons Dijon mustard
- 1 tablespoon chopped fresh thyme
- 4 pork chops (approximately 6 oz each)
- Salt and pepper to taste
- 1 tablespoon chopped fresh parsley

**Directions:**
1. Sprinkle salt and pepper over both sides of the pork chops.
2. Heat olive oil in a skillet over medium high heat.

3. Add the pork chops to the skillet and cook for about 45 minutes per side until they reach an internal temperature of 145°F (63°C).
4. Remove the pork chops from the skillet and let them rest on a plate.
5. In the same skillet, reduce the heat to medium low and add the heavy cream, Dijon mustard, chopped thyme, and chopped parsley. Stir well to combine.
6. Simmer the sauce for a few minutes until it thickens slightly.
7. Pour the mustard cream sauce over the pork chops before serving.

# Grilled Chicken Caesar Salad

**Ingredients:**

- Romaine lettuce

- Caesar dressing (without added sugars)

- 2 chicken breasts

- Grated Parmesan cheese (optional)

**Directions:**

1. Preheat a grill or skillet to mediumhigh heat.
2. Season the chicken breasts with salt and pepper.
3. Grill or cook the chicken breasts until fully cooked.
4. Slice the cooked chicken breasts and place them over a bed of romaine lettuce.

5. Drizzle Caesar dressing over the salad and sprinkle with grated Parmesan cheese if desired.

## Tuna Avocado Lettuce Wraps:

**Ingredients:**

- Lettuce leaves (such as romaine or iceberg)
- Salt and pepper to taste
- 1 can of tuna (in water or olive oil)
- 1 ripe avocado, mashed

**Directions:**
1. Drain the canned tuna and place it in a bowl.
2. Add the mashed avocado to the bowl and mix well.
3. Season the tuna and avocado mixture with salt and pepper.
4. Spoon the mixture onto lettuce leaves and wrap them up.
5. Enjoy the lettuce wraps as a refreshing and satisfying lunch.

# Ground Beef Lettuce Wraps

**Ingredients:**

- 1 pound ground beef

- Lettuce leaves (such as romaine or iceberg)

- Salt and pepper to taste

- Optional toppings: diced tomatoes, sliced avocado, chopped onions

**Directions:**
1. In a skillet, cook the ground beef over medium heat until browned and cooked through.
2. Season the ground beef with salt and pepper.
3. Spoon the cooked ground beef onto lettuce leaves.
4. Add optional toppings if desired.

5. Wrap the lettuce leaves around the ground beef to create lettuce wraps.
6. Enjoy the flavorful and lowcarb ground beef lettuce wraps.

# Chicken Bacon Ranch Salad

**Ingredients:**

- Grilled or roasted chicken breast, sliced Crispy bacon, crumbled

- Romaine lettuce

- Ranch dressing (without added sugars) Optional toppings: cherry tomatoes, sliced cucumbers, shredded cheese

**Directions:**

1. Arrange the sliced chicken breast, crumbled bacon, and romaine lettuce in a salad bowl.
2. Add optional toppings if desired.
3. Drizzle ranch dressing over the salad.
4. Toss to coat everything evenly.
5. Enjoy the delicious and satisfying chicken bacon ranch salad.

## Beef Patties

**Ingredients:**

- 2 tbsp. butter, melted
- 1 tsp. dried rosemary
- 1 tbsp. dried oregano
- 1 tbsp. dried thyme
- 1 tsp. pepper
- 1 lb. ground beef
- 1 lb. ground lamb
- 1 1/2 tsp. salt

**Directions:**

1. Add all Ingredients: into the large bowl and mix until well combined.

2. Make even shape patties from meat mixture.
3. Grill patties over medium heat for 5 minutes on each side.
4. Serve and enjoy.

# Simple Beef Roast

## Ingredients:

- 1 stick butter
- Pepper
- 5 lb. beef roast
- 2 tbsp. garlic, minced
- Salt

## Directions:
1. Place the beef roast into the slow cooker.
2. Sprinkle garlic, pepper, and salt over the roast.
3. Place butter on top of the roast.
4. Cover and cook on low for 10 hours.
5. Using a fork shred the meat.
6. Serve and enjoy.

## Roasted Sirloin Steak

**Ingredients:**

- 2 garlic cloves, minced

- 1/4 cup water

- 1/4 cup butter, melted

- 1/2 tsp. black pepper

- 1 tsp. dried oregano

- 2 lb. sirloin steak, cut into 1inch cubes

- 1 tsp. salt

**Directions:**
1. Add all Ingredients: except beef into the large bowl and mix well.
2. Pour bowl mixture into the large zip lock bag.

3. Add beef to the bag and shake well and place it in the refrigerator for 1 hour.
4. Preheat the oven to 400 F.
5. Place marinated beef on a baking tray and bake for 30 minutes.
6. Serve and enjoy.

# Beef Tacos

**Ingredients:**

- 1 1/2 lb. beef roast
- 1 cup beef stock
- Pepper
- Salt

**Directions:**
1. Place the beef roast into the instant pot.
2. Add remaining Ingredients: into the pot.
3. Secure pot with a lid and selects manual and cook for 60 minutes.
4. Once done release pressure using quick release then remove the lid.
5. Remove meat from pot and shred using a fork.
6. Serve and enjoy.

# Bacon Mayonnaise

**Ingredients:**

- 1 to 2 teaspoons freshly squeezed lemon juice or distilled white vinegar (optional)

- 1 cup bacon drippings, melted

- 1 whole large egg or 2 large egg yolks, at room temperature

- Sea salt

**Directions:**

1. Put the egg and lemon juice (if using) in a 12ounce widemouth jar or sealable cup.
2. Using an immersion blender, whip for 10 to 20 seconds.
3. Set the blender on low speed. Pour the warm bacon fat into the jar.

4. Move the blender up and down until all the fat is incorporated and the mixture is emulsified.
5. If it doesn't fully combine, allow it to sit for 10 minutes, add a few drops of water, and blend again. Season with salt.

# Duck Fat Mayonnaise

**Ingredients:**

- 1 teaspoon Dijon mustard

- 1 to 2 teaspoons freshly squeezed lemon juice or distilled white vinegar (optional)

- 1 cup duck fat, melted and warm

- 1 whole large egg or 2 large egg yolks, at room temperature

- Sea salt

**Directions:**

1. In a 12ounce widemouth jar or sealable cup, combine the egg, mustard, and lemon juice (if using). Using an immersion blender, blend on low speed.

2. Move the blender up and down while pouring the warm duck fat into the jar. Continue to

blend until all the fat is incorporated and the mayonnaise is emulsified.

3. If the mixture is not fully combined, let it sit for 10 minutes, add a few drops of water, and blend again. Season with salt.

## Easy Hollandaise Sauce

**Ingredients:**

- 1 to 2 tablespoons freshly squeezed lemon juice

- 8 tablespoons (1 stick) unsalted butter, melted

- Sea salt

- 3 large egg yolks, at room temperature

- Pinch cayenne pepper (optional)

**Directions:**

1. Put the egg yolks and lemon juice in a 12ounce widemouth jar. Using an immersion blender, blend until just combined.
2. Set the blender on low speed. With the blender touching the bottom of the jar, pour

in the warm butter in a continuous stream until combined, about 30 seconds.
3. Season with salt and cayenne pepper (if using). Serve immediately.

## Ovenboiled Eggs

**Ingredients:**

- 12 large eggs

**Directions:**

1. Preheat the oven to 325°F.
2. Place 1 egg into each cup of a 12cup muffin tin.
3. Transfer the muffin tin to the oven, and bake for 25 minutes. Remove from the oven.
4. Plunge the eggs into cold water to stop the cooking process.

## Perfect Bacon

**Ingredients:**

- 1½ pounds uncured bacon slices

**Directions:**

1. Line a platter with paper towels and set aside.
2. Lay the bacon slices ¼ inch apart on a baking sheet.
3. Transfer the baking sheet to a cold oven. Set the oven to 400°F. Bake for 20 to 30 minutes, or until the bacon reaches the desired level of crispness. Remove from the oven. Transfer the bacon to the prepared platter.

# Crispy Baked Chicken Wings With Red Cabbage Slaw

**Ingredients:**

- Salt and ground black pepper, to taste
- 1 head red cabbage, shredded
- 1 carrot, shredded
- 1/4 cup mayonnaise
- 2 tablespoons apple cider vinegar
- 2 tablespoons honey
- 2 lb. chicken wings
- 2 tablespoons olive oil
- 1 teaspoon garlic powder

- 1 teaspoon onion powder

- 1 teaspoon smoked paprika

- 2 tablespoons fresh chopped parsley

**Directions:**

1. Preheat oven to 425°F and line a large baking sheet with parchment paper.
2. In a large bowl, combine chicken wings, olive oil, garlic powder, onion powder, smoked paprika, salt, and pepper.
3. Toss to combine and spread wings out evenly on the prepared baking sheet.
4. Bake for 20 minutes, flipping wings halfway through.
5. While wings are baking, combine shredded cabbage, carrot, mayonnaise, apple cider vinegar, honey, and parsley in a large bowl. Toss to combine and set aside.

6. When wings are done baking, remove from oven and serve with red cabbage slaw. Enjoy!

## Baked Salmon With Avocado Salsa

**Ingredients:**

- 2 tablespoons diced red onion

- 1 tablespoon diced jalapeno

- 2 tablespoons diced fresh cilantro

- 2 tablespoons lime juice

- 4 skinless salmon fillets

- 1 teaspoon olive oil

- 2 avocados, diced

- Salt and pepper, to taste

**Directions:**

1. Preheat oven to 375°F.
2. Rinse salmon fillets, pat dry and place on a greased baking sheet.
3. Drizzle olive oil over the salmon fillets and season with salt and pepper.
4. Bake in preheated oven for 10 minutes, or until cooked through.
5. Meanwhile, in a bowl combine diced avocados, red onion, jalapeno, cilantro, and lime juice.
6. Season with salt and pepper to taste.
7. Serve salmon with the avocado salsa on top. Enjoy!

# Pan Seared Pork Chops With Garlic And Herbs

## Ingredients:

- 2 cloves garlic, minced
- 2 teaspoons fresh rosemary, chopped
- 2 teaspoons fresh thyme, chopped
- 4 pork chops
- 2 tablespoons olive oil
- Salt and pepper, to taste

## Directions:

1. Heat the olive oil in a large skillet over medium high heat.
2. Add the pork chops to the skillet and season with salt and pepper.

3. Cook for 56 minutes per side, or until golden brown and cooked through.
4. Reduce the heat to medium low and add the garlic, rosemary and thyme.
5. Cook for an additional minute, stirring occasionally, until the herbs are fragrant.
6. Serve the pork chops hot with your favorite sides. Enjoy!

## Zucchini Rolls With Ham And Cheese

**Ingredients:**

- 4 slices of prosciutto
- Fresh cheese to taste
- Olive oil
- 2 medium zucchini
- Salt and pepper to taste.

**Directions:**
1. Preheat the oven to 200°C. Trim the ends of the zucchini and cut them into long, thin slices lengthwise.
2. Brush the zucchini slices with a drizzle of olive oil and season with salt and pepper.

3. Arrange a slice of prosciutto on each zucchini slice and add a little cheese on top of the prosciutto.
4. Roll the zucchini slices with the ham and cheese inside, forming rolls.
5. Place the zucchini rolls on a baking sheet and bake them in the preheated oven for about 10 to 12 minutes, until the zucchini is soft and the ham is crispy.
6. Once cooked, transfer the zucchini rolls to a serving platter and serve warm as an appetizer or side dish.

## Cooked Ham With Fresh Figs

**Ingredients:**

- Cheese to taste (such as
- goat cheese or gorgonzola)
- Honey to taste
- 8 slices of cooked ham
- 4 fresh figs, cut in half
- Arugula (optional)

**Directions:**

1. Arrange the ham slices on a serving platter. Place a fig half on each ham slice.
2. Add a little cheese on top of each fig. You can also add a drizzle of honey over the figs and cheese for a touch of sweetness.

3. If you wish, you can add a bed of arugula on the serving platter and place the slices of cooked ham with figs on top.
4. Serve the cooked ham with fresh figs as an appetizer or as part of a mixed salad.

## Grilled Sausages With Mustard

**Ingredients:**

- 4 tablespoons of mustard

- 2 tablespoons honey

- 1 tablespoon olive oil

- 8 sausages (you can choose the type

- of sausage you prefer)

- Salt and pepper to taste.

**Directions:**

1. Preheat the grill or barbecue to medium high temperature. In a small bowl, mix mustard, honey, olive oil, salt, and pepper.
2. Brush the sausages with the mustard mixture and place them on the preheated grill.
3. Cook the sausages for 5 to 7 minutes per side, or until they are well cooked and have nice grilled streaks.
4. While cooking, brush the sausages with some of the remaining mustard mixtures to intensify the flavor.
5. Once cooked, remove the sausages from the grill and let them rest for a few minutes.
6. Serve the grilled sausages with mustard accompanied by side dishes of your choice, such as bread, chips, or grilled vegetables.

**Bacon And Cheese Omelet**

**Ingredients:**

- 100 g grated cheese

- Salt and pepper to taste

- 4 slices of smoked bacon

- 4 eggs

- 1/4 cup of milk

- 2 tablespoons olive oil

**Directions:**
1. In a nonstick skillet, cook the smoked bacon until crispy. Once cooked, drain it on paper towels to remove excess fat and cut it into small pieces. In a bowl, beat the eggs with the

milk. Add the grated cheese, chopped bacon, salt and pepper.
2. Mix all the Ingredients: well. Heat the olive oil in the same skillet in which you cooked the bacon.
3. Pour the egg mixture into the pan and distribute it evenly. Cook the frittata over medium low heat for 10 to 15 minutes, or until it is well set on the edges and slightly soft in the center.
4. When the frittata is ready, shake it gently in the skillet to make sure it does not stick.
5. Using a lid or plate, flip the frittata oven to cook the other side as well.
6. Cook it for another 2 to 3 minutes. Transfer the frittata to a serving plate and cut it into wedges. Serve warm.

## Cauliflower Rice

**Ingredients:**

- 2 tablespoons olive oil

- 1 head of cauliflower

- Salt and pepper to taste

**Directions:**

1. Wash and dry the cauliflower head thoroughly.
2. Cut the cauliflower into florets, removing the tough core.
3. Place the cauliflower florets in a food processor and pulse until they are finely chopped and resemble rice grains.
4. In a skillet over medium heat, heat the olive oil.
5. Add the cauliflower rice to the skillet and sauté it for 34 minutes or until it's tender crisp.
6. Season the Cauliflower Rice with salt and pepper to taste.

7. Serve the cauliflower rice as a low carb and nutritious alternative to traditional rice.

## Baconwrapped Asparagus

**Ingredients:**

- 6 slices of bacon
- 12 asparagus spears

**Directions:**
1. Preheat your oven to 400°F (200°C) and line a baking sheet with parchment paper.
2. Trim the tough ends of the asparagus spears.
3. Take a slice of bacon and wrap it around each asparagus spear, starting from the bottom and spiraling up to the tip.
4. Place the prosciutto wrapped asparagus on the prepared baking sheet.
5. Bake in the preheated oven for 1012 minutes or until the asparagus is tender and the prosciutto is crispy.

6. Remove the Prosciutto Wrapped Asparagus from the oven and serve immediately. Enjoy this elegant and flavorful appetizer!

## Creamed Spinach

**Ingredients:**

- 4 tablespoons butter
- 1/4 cup heavy cream
- Salt and pepper to taste
- 2 bunches of fresh spinach, washed and stems removed
- Grated Parmesan cheese (optional)

**Directions:**
1. In a large pot or skillet over medium heat, melt the butter.
2. Add the washed spinach to the pot and cook it until it wilts down.
3. Pour in the heavy cream and stir to combine.
4. Cook the Creamed Spinach for another 23 minutes, allowing the flavors to meld.

5. Season the creamed spinach with salt and pepper to taste.
6. If desired, sprinkle grated Parmesan cheese over the creamed spinach before serving. Enjoy this rich and comforting side dish!

# Bacon Wrapped Pork Chops

**INGREDIENTS:**

- 2 teaspoons of olive oil
- 2 tablespoons of butter
- 2 garlic cloves, minced
- 4 thick cut boneless pork chops
- 8 strips of bacon
- Salt and pepper
- 1 teaspoon of dried thyme

**DIRECTIONS:**

1. Preheat the oven to 400°F (205°C).
2. Season each pork chop with salt and pepper on both sides.

3. Take two bacon strips and wrap them around each pork chop, securing with toothpicks if necessary.
4. Heat the olive oil in a large oven safe skillet over medium high heat.
5. Once hot, add the pork chops and sear on each side for 23 minutes until browned.
6. Remove the pork chops from the skillet and set them aside.
7. Reduce the heat to medium and add the butter, garlic, and thyme to the skillet. Cook for 12 minutes until fragrant.
8. Return the pork chops to the skillet, basting them with the garlic butter.
9. Place the skillet in the preheated oven and bake for 1520 minutes, or until the internal temperature of the pork reaches 145°F (63°C).
10. Remove the skillet from the oven and let the pork chops rest for 5 minutes before serving. Enjoy!

## Slow Cooked Beef Brisket

**INGREDIENTS:**

- 1 tbsp paprika

- 1 tbsp chili powder

- 1 tbsp cumin

- 1 tbsp dried thyme

- 2 cups beef broth

- 1 (45 lb) beef brisket

- 2 tbsp salt

- 2 tbsp black pepper

- 2 tbsp garlic powder

- 2 tbsp onion powder

**Directions:**
1. Preheat the oven to 275°F (135°C).
2. In a small bowl, mix together salt, black pepper, garlic powder, onion powder, paprika, chili powder, cumin, and thyme.
3. Rub the seasoning mixture generously onto all sides of the beef brisket.
4. Place the beef brisket in a large roasting pan or Dutch oven.
5. Pour the beef broth over the brisket, covering it as much as possible.
6. Cover the roasting pan or Dutch oven with a lid or tightly sealed foil.
7. Place the pan in the oven and cook for 45 hours or until the brisket is forktender.
8. Once cooked, remove the brisket from the pan and let it rest for 1015 minutes before slicing it.

9. Serve the sliced brisket with some of the juices from the pan poured over the top.
10. Enjoy your slow cooked beef brisket as a hearty and satisfying meal that's perfect for a carnivore diet!

## Herb Crusted Lamb Chops

**INGREDIENTS:**

- 2 tablespoons chopped fresh rosemary

- 2 tablespoons chopped fresh thyme

- 2 tablespoons chopped fresh parsley

- 2 cloves garlic, minced

- Salt and pepper

- 4 lamb chops, about 1inch thick

- 1/2 cup breadcrumbs

- 2 tablespoons olive oil

**DIRECTIONS:**

1. Preheat the oven to 400°F.

2. In a small bowl, mix together the breadcrumbs, rosemary, thyme, parsley, garlic, salt, and pepper.
3. Brush the lamb chops with olive oil and season them with salt and pepper.
4. Press the breadcrumb mixture onto both sides of the lamb chops, making sure to coat them evenly.
5. Heat a large skillet over medium high heat. Add the lamb chops to the skillet and cook for 34 minutes on each side, or until nicely browned.
6. Transfer the skillet to the preheated oven and bake for an additional 1012 minutes, or until the lamb chops are cooked to your desired doneness.
7. Remove the lamb chops from the oven and let them rest for 5 minutes before serving.
8. Serve the lamb chops with your favorite sides, such as roasted vegetables or a simple salad.

# Steak And Egg Breakfast Salad

**Ingredients:**

- 1/4 red onion, thinly sliced

- 1/2 avocado, sliced

- 2 tbsp. olive oil

- 1 tbsp. balsamic vinegar

- 1 (8 oz.) steak, cooked and sliced

- 2 eggs

- 2 cups mixed salad greens

- Salt and pepper

**Directions:**

1. Heat a skillet over medium high heat and cook the steak to your desired doneness. Leave it for 12 minutes before slicing.
2. Meanwhile, in another skillet, cook the eggs to your liking (fried or scrambled).
3. In a mixing bowl, whisk together the olive oil, balsamic vinegar, salt, and pepper to make a dressing.
4. In a salad bowl, mix together the mixed greens, red onion, and avocado.
5. Toss to coat by drizzling the dressing.
6. Add the sliced steak and cooked eggs on top of the salad.
7. Serve immediately.

## Bun Less Bacon Cheeseburger

**Ingredients:**

- 1 slice of cheese

- Salt and pepper

- 8 oz. ground beef

- 2 slices of bacon

- Butter

**Directions:**

1. Preheat a skillet over medium heat.
2. Form the ground beef into a patty and season with salt and pepper.
3. Melt a tablespoon of butter in the skillet and add the ground beef patty.
4. Cook the patty for 34 minutes on each side, or until browned and cooked through.

5. While the patty is cooking, fry the bacon in a separate skillet until crispy.
6. Once the patty is cooked, add the cheese on top and let it melt.
7. Serve the patty on a plate and top with the bacon slices.

## Salmon And Cream Cheese Breakfast Wrap

**Ingredients:**

- 2 oz. cream cheese

- 1 lowcarb wrap (or lettuce leaves for a lowcarb option)

- 1 tbsp. butter

- 1 salmon filet

- 2 large eggs

- Salt and pepper

**Directions:**
1. Preheat a skillet over medium high heat.
2. Season the salmon filet with salt and pepper and add it to the skillet.
3. Cook the salmon for 34 minutes on each side, or until cooked through.

4. Melt the butter over low heat, in another skillet,
5. Beat the eggs in a mixing bowl and season with salt and pepper. Put the eggs in the skillet and scramble until cooked properly.
6. Spread the cream cheese on the wrap (or lettuce leaves).
7. Add the cooked salmon and scrambled eggs on top of the cream cheese.
8. Roll up the wrap (or wrap the lettuce leaves around the filling).
9. Serve hot.

## Grilled Steak With Roasted Vegetables

**Ingredients:**

- 1 tablespoon olive oil

- Assorted vegetables (e.g., bell peppers, zucchini, onions, mushrooms)

- 2 steaks (such as Rib eye or sirloin)

- Salt and pepper to taste

- Garlic powder and dried herbs (optional)

**Directions:**
1. Preheat the grill to medium high heat.
2. Season the steaks with salt and pepper on both sides.
3. Drizzle the steaks with olive oil and rub it in to coat evenly.

4. Place the steaks on the grill and cook for 46 minutes per side, or until desired doneness is reached.
5. While the steaks are grilling, prepare the roasted vegetables.
6. Cut the assorted vegetables into bite sized pieces and place them on a baking sheet.
7. Drizzle the vegetables with olive oil and season with salt, pepper, garlic powder, and dried herbs (if desired).
8. Roast the vegetables in the oven at 425°F (220°C) for about 2025 minutes, or until they are tender and slightly caramelized.
9. Remove the steaks from the grill and let them rest for a few minutes before slicing.
10. Serve the grilled steak with the roasted vegetables for a delicious and satisfying main dish.

## Baked Lemon Herb Chicken

**Ingredients:**

- 1 teaspoon dried thyme
- 1 teaspoon dried rosemary
- Salt and pepper to taste
- 4 boneless, skinless chicken breasts
- Juice of 1 lemon
- 2 tablespoons olive oil
- 2 cloves garlic, minced
- Fresh parsley for garnish (optional)

**Directions:**

1. Preheat the oven to 400°F (200°C).

2. In a small bowl, whisk together the lemon juice, olive oil, minced garlic, dried thyme, dried rosemary, salt, and pepper.
3. Place the chicken breasts in a baking dish and pour the lemon herb mixture over them, ensuring they are coated evenly.
4. Bake in the preheated oven for 2025 minutes or until the chicken is cooked through and no longer pink in the center.
5. Remove from the oven and let the chicken rest for a few minutes.
6. Garnish with fresh parsley if desired.
7. Serve the baked lemon herb chicken with your favorite side dishes.

## Salmon With Lemon Dill Sauce

**Ingredients:**

- 2 tablespoons olive oil
- Juice of 1 lemon
- 1/4 cup mayonnaise
- 1 tablespoon fresh dill, chopped
- 4 salmon fillets
- Salt and pepper to taste
- 1 clove garlic, minced

**Directions:**
1. Preheat the oven to 425°F (220°C).
2. Season the salmon fillets with salt and pepper on both sides.

3. Heat olive oil in an oven safe skillet over medium high heat.
1. Place the salmon fillets in the skillet and sear for 23 minutes on each side.
4. Transfer the skillet to the preheated oven and bake for an additional 810 minutes or until the salmon is cooked to your liking.
5. While the salmon is baking, prepare the lemon dill sauce.
6. In a small bowl, combine the lemon juice, mayonnaise, fresh dill, and minced garlic. Stir well to combine.
7. Remove the salmon from the oven and let it rest for a few minutes.
8. Serve the salmon fillets with a dollop of lemon dill sauce on top.

## Beef Stir Fry With Vegetables

**Ingredients:**

- 1 tablespoon cornstarch

- 2 tablespoons cooking oil

- 2 cloves garlic, minced

- 1 teaspoon grated ginger

- Assorted vegetables (e.g., broccoli, bell peppers, carrots, snap peas)

- 1 pound beef (such as sirloin or flank steak), thinly sliced

- 2 tablespoons soy sauce

- 1 tablespoon oyster sauce

- Salt and pepper to taste

**Directions:**
1. In a bowl, whisk together the soy sauce, oyster sauce, and cornstarch to make a marinade.
2. Add the thinly sliced beef to the marinade and let it marinate for 15-20 minutes.
3. Heat the cooking oil in a large skillet or wok over high heat.
4. Add the minced garlic and grated ginger to the skillet and stir fry for 1 minute until fragrant.
5. Add the marinated beef to the skillet and stir fry for 2-3 minutes until it is browned and cooked through.
6. Remove the beef from the skillet and set it aside.
7. In the same skillet, add the assorted vegetables and stir fry for 3-4 minutes until they are crisp tender.

8. Return the beef to the skillet and stir everything together.
9. Season with salt and pepper to taste.

# Crispy Baked Chicken Wings

**Ingredients:**

- 2 tablespoons of olive oil
- 2 cloves of garlic
- 1 teaspoon of dried oregano
- 2 lbs of chicken wings
- Salt and pepper to taste

**Directions:**
1. Preheat oven to 425°F.
2. Place chicken wings in a large bowl and drizzle with olive oil, garlic, oregano, salt, and pepper.
3. Place the chicken wings on a greased baking sheet.

4. Bake in the preheated oven for 2530 minutes, or until chicken is cooked through and golden brown.
5. Let the chicken wings rest for a few minutes before serving. Enjoy!

## Bbq Ribs

**Ingredients:**

- 2 tablespoons of olive oil
- 2 cloves of garlic
- 1 teaspoon of dried oregano
- 2 racks of pork ribs
- 1 cup of your favorite BBQ sauce
- Salt and pepper to taste

**Directions:**
1. Preheat oven to 375°F.
2. Rub the ribs with the olive oil, garlic, oregano, salt, and pepper.
3. Place the ribs on a greased baking sheet.
4. Bake in the preheated oven for 1 hour.

5. Remove from the oven and brush with BBQ sauce.
6. Place the ribs back in the oven for an additional 15 minutes.
7. Let the ribs rest for a few minutes before serving. Enjoy!

## Grilled Sausages

**Ingredients:**

- 2 cloves of garlic
- 1 teaspoon of dried oregano
- 8 sausages
- 2 tablespoons of olive oil
- Salt and pepper to taste

**Directions:**

1. Preheat your grill to medium heat (or a skillet to medium heat if you don't have a grill).
2. Rub the sausages with the olive oil, garlic, oregano, salt, and pepper.
3. Place the sausages on the preheated grill (or skillet) and cook for 810 minutes, or until cooked through.

4. Let the sausages rest for a few minutes before serving. Enjoy!

## Classic Rib Eye Lettuce Wraps

**Ingredients:**

- Rib eye steak (preferably grass-fed and pasture raised)

- Large lettuce leaves (such as romaine, iceberg, or butter lettuce)

- Salt and pepper to taste

**Directions:**

1. Preheat your grill or stovetop griddle to high heat.
2. Season the rib eye steak generously with salt and pepper on both sides.
3. Grill the rib eye steak for approximately 45 minutes per side, or until it reaches your desired level of doneness.

4. Remove the rib eye steak from the grill and let it rest for a few minutes to allow the juices to redistribute.
5. Slice the rib eye steak into thin strips, ensuring it is tender and juicy.
6. Lay out the large lettuce leaves on a clean surface.
7. Place the sliced rib eye steak on each lettuce leaf, creating individual wraps.
8. Roll up the lettuce leaves with the rib eye steak inside, securing them with a toothpick if necessary.
9. Serve the classic Rib eye lettuce wraps as a delectable and protein packed main course or appetizer.

## Garlic Butter Rib Eye Lettuce Wraps

**Ingredients:**

- Large lettuce leaves (such as romaine, iceberg, or butter lettuce)
- Garlic butter (homemade or storebought)
- Fresh parsley (for garnish)
- Rib eye steak (preferably grassfed and pastureraised)
- Salt and pepper to taste

**Directions:**

1. Preheat your grill or stovetop griddle to high heat.
2. Season the Rib eye steak with salt and pepper on both sides.

3. Grill the Rib eye steak for approximately 45 minutes per side, or until it reaches your desired level of doneness.
4. Remove the Rib eye steak from the grill and let it rest for a few minutes.
5. Slice the Rib eye steak into thin strips and toss them in a generous amount of garlic butter while still warm.
6. Lay out the large lettuce leaves on a clean surface.
7. Place the garlic buttercoated Rib eye strips on each lettuce leaf, creating flavorful and indulgent wraps.
8. Roll up the lettuce leaves with the garlic butter Rib eye inside, securing them with toothpicks if needed.
9. Garnish the garlic butter Rib eye lettuce wraps with fresh parsley for a burst of color and flavor.

10. Serve the irresistible garlic butter Rib eye lettuce wraps as a satisfying and nourishing main course or appetizer.

## Asian Inspired Rib Eye Lettuce Wraps

**Ingredients:**

- Coconut aminos or tamari sauce (a soy sauce alternative)

- Fresh ginger (grated)

- Fresh green onions (sliced)

- Sesame seeds (for garnish)

- Rib eye steak (preferably grassfed and pastureraised)

- Large lettuce leaves (such as romaine, iceberg, or butter lettuce)

- Sesame oil

- Salt and pepper to taste

**Directions:**

1. Preheat your grill or stovetop griddle to high heat.
2. Season the Rib eye steak with salt and pepper on both sides.
3. Grill the Rib eye steak for approximately 45 minutes per side, or until it reaches your desired level of doneness.
4. Remove the Rib eye steak from the grill and let it rest for a few minutes.
5. Slice the Rib eye steak into thin strips, ensuring tenderness and juiciness.
6. In a bowl, combine sesame oil, coconut amines or tamari sauce, grated ginger, and sliced green onions to create a savory and aromatic marinade.
7. Toss the Rib eye strips in the Asian inspired marinade, allowing the flavors to meld for a few minutes.
8. Lay out the large lettuce leaves on a clean surface.

9. Place the marinated Rib eye strips on each lettuce leaf, infusing them with the delectable Asian inspired flavors.
10. Roll up the lettuce leaves with the Asian marinated Rib eye inside, garnishing the wraps with sesame seeds for added texture and appeal.
11. Serve the mouthwatering Asian inspired Rib eye lettuce wraps as a flavorful and satisfying main course or appetizer.

# Bacon Wrapped Dates

**Ingredients:**

- 12 large dates
- 12 slices bacon
- toothpicks

**Directions:**
1. Preheat oven to 200°C (400°F).
2. Each date should have its pit removed by making a longitudinal cut.
3. Each date should be wrapped in a piece of bacon and fastened with a toothpick.
4. On a baking sheet with parchment paper, arrange the dates that have been wrapped in bacon.
5. Bake the bacon for 15 to 20 minutes, or until it is crispy.

# Deviled Eggs With Bacon

**Ingredients:**

- 1 tbsp Dijon mustard
- 1/4 tsp garlic powder
- 1/4 tsp onion powder
- salt and black pepper, to taste
- 6 hardboiled eggs
- 2 tbsp mayonnaise
- 2 slices bacon, cooked and crumbled

**Directions:**

1. The yolks should be removed after cutting the hardboiled eggs in half lengthwise.
2. In a bowl, mix together the egg yolks, mayonnaise, Dijon mustard, garlic powder,

onion powder, salt, and black pepper until smooth.
3. Refill the egg white halves with the mixture by spooning.
4. Top each deviled egg with crumbled bacon.

# Garlic Butter Shrimp

**Ingredients:**

- 2 tbsp butter

- 2 cloves garlic, minced

- 1 pound shrimp, peeled and deveined

- salt and black pepper, to taste

**Directions:**
1. Butter should be melted in a large pan over a medium heat.
2. Add the minced garlic and simmer for a few minutes, until fragrant.
3. Cook the shrimp in the pan for two to three minutes on each side, or until pink and fully cooked.
4. To flavor, add salt & black chilli to the dish.

## Grilled Chicken Caesar Salad With Bacon

**Ingredients:**

- 4 cooked and crumbled slices of bacon

- Romaine lettuce, chopped

- Caesar dressing (look for one without added sugars)

- Salt and pepper to taste

- 1 tablespoon olive oil

- Parmesan cheese, shaved or grated

**Directions:**

1. Grill the chicken breasts for about 67 minutes per side until cooked through and no longer pink in the center. The thickness of the chicken breasts may affect the amount of time needed to cook them.

2. Remove the chicken breasts from the grill and let them rest for a few minutes before slicing.
3. In a large bowl, combine chopped romaine lettuce, crumbled bacon, and Caesar dressing. Toss to coat the lettuce evenly.
4. Divide the salad onto plates and top with sliced grilled chicken.
5. Garnish with shaved or grated Parmesan cheese before serving.

www.ingramcontent.com/pod-product-compliance
Lightning Source LLC
LaVergne TN
LVHW010222070526
838199LV00062B/4687